Routes, Roads, Regiments

and Rebellions

COLIN MCCALL is a former teacher, educational psychologist, university tutor and civil servant. He now works as a freelance research and development consultant in the fields of education and training. His love of the outdoors, more especially fell walking, and his general interest in history and historical biography have combined to sustain for more than a decade a wish to trace the fascinating life of General George Wade. Although already an author of published works on educational topics, this is his first journey into writing about historical legacy.

Routes, Roads, Regiments and Rebellions

A brief history of the life and work of
General George Wade (1673–1748)
the Father of the Military Roads in Scotland

written by
Colin McCall
Illustrated by
Martin Wellard

Lesser Known Heroes

SOLCOL

Copyright © Colin McCall 2003
Illustrations © Martin Wellard 2003
First published in 2003 by SOLCOL
6 Moorcroft, Chesterfield Rd
Matlock, Derbyshire DE4 5LL

Distributed by Gazelle Book Services Limited
Hightown, White Cross Mills, South Rd
Lancaster, England LA1 4XS

British Library Cataloguing in Publication Data
A catalogue record for this book is available from the British
Library

ISBN 0-9544455-0-3

Typeset by Amolibros, Milverton, Somerset
This book production has been managed by Amolibros
Printed and bound by Advance Book Printing Ltd

Contents

List of Illustrations

In the text

Acknowledgements

I WOULD like to thank the following for their encouragement and support. For love, life, and listening to endless snippets about George Wade, Margaret, Charlotte and Richard McCall. 'At last I have painted my Highland journey.' Martin Wellard for his beautiful sketches and for bearing with me when it was not clear what I wanted and where we might obtain it. For general help and advice, The British Library and Derby Museum and Art Gallery. Charlotte McCall and Tom Davis for help with field work in Scotland. Those who seek to preserve the wild, uninhabited and uncultivated regions of the world. I hope they will enjoy this little book. It is in such geographical areas that succeeding generations have the best chance to learn that 'experiences not found in the normal course of life often turn out to be the best'.

Colin McCall, Matlock, Derbyshire,
December 2002.

 *Preamble*

THE NAMES of the principal characters and the locations that appear in this text have different spellings across both the classical historical evidence and the more recent sources of information. For example, William Caulfeild appears as both Caulfeild and Caulfield, and references to the Corrieyairack Road and Pass come with at least three different spellings. I have standardised on Caulfield and Corrieyairack, excepting where there is a different presentation in a specific historical source. Here my belief that Old English should not be treated with disdain leads me to retain the authentic representation.

Likewise, some of the written sources examined in the course of preparing the book, are referenced accurately and in full. Others I can provide only in part. This is how it seems to be in much of the literature currently available. However, there is no suggestion that this brief work is a full academic treatise. It is hoped that others may write more extensively and more analytically about the period and the lead character. That said, I do hope that any reader who wishes to undertake a fuller exploration of George Wade and his achievements will have sufficient guidance in what I have been able to provide to make a good start.

From time to time I have suspended the main commentary on George in order to set out in more detail some related personalities or events. I have called these links 'historical connections' and I hope they will be of interest to the reader. They serve to place George Wade within a broader picture of past and present circumstances.

Introduction

GEORGE WADE was a visionary, a competent observer of social and political circumstances, a good and steady soldier, a builder genius, a philanthropic MP and a wise and conciliatory man. He retained a good measure of personal popularity in the pre-1745 Scottish Highlands, despite having to heed many disagreeable orders. He fulfilled the duties expected of him, but saw beyond the narrow confines of their strict interpretation.

In the course of his adventurous and, at times, hazardous life, Wade held steadfast to his responsibilities, whether military or civil. His greatest achievement was destined to take shape in the Highlands of Scotland, and it was here that he found most solace and where he did his most purposeful work.

In partnership with his right-hand man, William Caulfield, he was to see take shape a network of roads for military transportation that ultimately did much more than transport soldier companies to control or fight restless clansmen. The roads helped the Highlanders to learn of places and ways beyond their mountains and glens, and they helped move other folk into the region to learn about the Highlanders' points of view. Today the remnants of the roads remain intriguing, challenging and worthwhile highways, both to the intrepid explorer and the lover of natural panoramas and mountainous majesty.

> Two hundred years ago George Wade
> For war built bridge and highway.
> Now Commerce finer roads has made,
> But I'll keep Wade's for my way.
> For when you and I went wandering
> We knew all tumult cease.
> And birds and beasts had mind for us
> And suns and stars were kind to us
> And we were glad to find for us
> Wade's quiet ways of peace.

Poem 'For Margaret', J E Salmond, 1934.

So let this little book tell how a man born in Killavalley in Ireland, who fought for military victories in places as far apart as Steinkirk in Flanders and Almanzain in Portugal, and who served as an MP in two English constituencies, eventually came to spend about ten years of his life overseeing a road-building programme through the rugged and desolate seventeenth-century Highland landscape.

*1 Field Marshall George Wade,
the father of the military roads,
by Johann van Diest.
(Reproduced with permission from the Scottish National
Portrait Gallery.)*

Roots
to
routes

WADE'S BIRTH in Ireland was in no small measure
due to Oliver Cromwell. Cromwell granted George's
grandfather, William Wade, land in West Meath and
King's County in lieu of payment for military services.
William's own son, Jerome, settled in Killavalley and his
three sons went one to the church, one to the estate
and one to the army, a not uncommon distribution in
those days for sons of the gentry. George's elder brother
William became canon of Windsor; Jerome his second
brother succeeded his father at Killavalley, while George
himself was gazetted an ensign in the earl of Bath's 10th
Foot regiment on 26th December 1690.

By all historical accounts, the young Wade is
recognised as a loyal and courageous officer. He was a
captain by 1675 and after distinguished service at the
siege of Liege, where with his grenadiers he charged
and took the citadel, he became a lieutenant colonel in
1703. He was a member of Lord Galway's expedition to

Portugal and again distinguished himself at the battle of Almanzain in 1707.

After a brief respite in England in 1708 and a further promotion to brigadier general, Wade joined General Stanhope's Minorca expedition. In the course of this sojourn, the troops encountered hilly and rocky terrain and found no roads of any quality. Stanhope's aide-de-camp mentions in his record that the troops, 'made a very good road for the canon' (quoted in Salmond, 1934) and if not directly in charge of this temporary road-making, Wade would certainly have witnessed the effort and the result. In 1710, Wade further distinguished himself at the battle of Saragossa.

Historical connection 1

In May 1710, Philip V of France assembled troops at Lerida on the western frontier of Catalonia. The force numbered about 22,000 men. Against them was an allied army of 24,000. These were mainly Spanish and Portuguese troops, but 4,200 were British, 1,400 German and 1,400 Dutch. Philip was surprised at Almenara on 27th July and the allies inflicted losses on him of 1,000 killed or wounded. The allies then pressed forward to Saragossa in north-eastern Spain. There, on 19th August, a battle was fought under the walls of the city. It ended in the complete rout of the

> Bourbon army. Three thousand men were killed or wounded, twenty cannon and sixty-three colours seized, and 4,000 prisoners were taken. The allies lost 2,000.

After Saragossa, Wade went on the retired list in 1711. His political career began shortly thereafter, when he was returned as MP for Hindon in Wiltshire.

At the outbreak of the 1715 Jacobite incursion, Wade commanded two regiments of dragoons in Bath. Here, by discovering hidden munitions and a surreptitious plot, he significantly enhanced his reputation in the eyes of King George I. Wade's find of weapons included

> eleven chests of fire-arms, swords, cartridges, three pieces of canon, one mortar and molds to cast canon.
>
> *Salmond, 1934.*

On the night of 29th January 1716, he also extracted by force papers in the possession of Count Gyllenborg, an ambassador from Sweden, who was a member of the English court. These papers revealed the involvement of the king of Sweden in a plot to bring back exiled Stewarts, thereby removing the Hanoverians from the British throne. For his success in handling these circumstantial events, Wade received the colonelcy of the

Third Dragoon Guards and a post of second in command of the 1719 expedition to Vigo.

His political career resumed in 1722 when he was elected MP for Bath. During his time in the city, various philanthropic deeds are registered to his credit. These include subscriptions to the Church of St Michael, the leadership of a range of charitable activities, and a not insignificant contribution to slum clearance.

Historical connection 2

Wade was an MP at a time when 'election' meant 'choice' not 'representation'. He would certainly not have been 'absolutely elected' by the local inhabitants, since electoral franchise was not then extensive and what did exist was limited to the male sex. It is more likely that the county sheriff or city officer asked him to stand, or a local committee or governing body of some standing nominated him for the role.

He would not have attended the now familiar Westminster House of Commons, because the current Houses of Parliament were not completed until 1867. Parliamentary business in his time was conducted at St Stephen's Chapel. This chapel was used for meetings of the House of Commons from 1547 until its destruction by fire in October 1834.

> Wade's tenure as MP overlapped with Robert Walpole's transformation of English parliamentary life. Because Walpole feared a resurgence of Jacobitism as much as the crown did, the two men collaborated in its prevention.

⁕

Wade may well have become more fully immersed in politics and his Bath constituency, but for a fateful influence upon his life, begun in 1724 by one Simon Fraser, Lord Lovat. In that year, Fraser sent a memorial to George I describing harsh clanship, ensuing conflicts and the trials of the general living conditions apparent to his eye in the Scottish Highlands.

Although regarded by most historical commentators as a memorial written predominantly to serve Fraser's own self-improvement, the content referred to events and misdemeanours to which George I could not turn a blind eye. Fraser spoke of

> 'quarrels and jealousies among the chiefs' leading to 'continual robberies and depredations in the Highlands', made worse by the 'mountainous situation of these parts, their remoteness from towns' such that 'criminals cannot be found by any methods now practical, much less seized and brought to justice'

resulting in them 'drawing many into their gangs who would otherwise be good subjects', thus collectively remaining 'ready and proper materials for disturbing the government upon the first occasion' with the people now forced to pay tribute to chieftains for protection through the fast spreading custom of 'Black Meal', from which comes the longer-lasting English equivalent 'blackmail'.

Lovat's memorial is published in full in an appendix to Burt's Letters *(fifth edition).*

3 *'Black Meal' in action.*

At the time George I received Fraser's memorial, Major George Wade was without a command, though he was probably sent to Scotland primarily because the king's advisers thought him able to visit the territory and report objectively on the state of things, particularly the accuracy of Fraser's ministrations. Thus, Wade went to

> inspect the situations of the Highlanders, their manners, customs, and the state of the country in regard to depredations said to be committed in that part of his Majesty's dominions... to report how far Fraser's Memorial was founded on fact, and whether his proposed remedies might properly be applied, and suggest to the king such other remedies as may conduce to the quiet of his Majesty's faithful subjects, and the good settlement of that part of the Kingdom.
>
> *Quoted in Salmond, 1934.*

Wade wasted little time. Setting out for Scotland on 4th July 1724, he dates his report on 10th December of the same year. He provides statistics on the men capable of bearing arms, 22,000 – of whom only

> '10,000 are well affected by the Government.' The rest he presumes 'have been engaged in Rebellion against Your Majesty and are ready...

to create new Troubles and raise Arms in favour of the Pretender'.

Wade's report is printed as an appendix to Burt's Letters *(fifth edition).*

Wade's report did concur with some of Lord Lovat's concerns. In particular, Wade agreed that the existing military barracks were not effective. They were under strength and two of the four were badly sited – 'not built in a proper situation as they might have been'. Equally, movement of troops and equipment was constrained, as the 'Highlands are still more impracticable, from the want of roads and bridges'.

Wade proposed a fort at Inverness and a new fort at Killichuimen. To service the latter with men and provisions, he suggested a small sailing ship on Loch Ness – a not altogether original idea, for Oliver Cromwell had put a vessel on the Ness. Naturally, however, given improvements in knowledge, skills and materials over time, Wade's *Highland Galley* was larger and more capable than Cromwell's earlier boat. His specifications were:

That a small vessel with Oars and Sails be built on the Lake Ness, sufficient to carry a Party of 60 or 80 Soldiers and Provisions for the Garrison, which will be a Means to keep the Communication open between that place and Inverness and be a safe and ready way of sending Parties to the Country bordering on the said Lake, which is Navigable for the largest Vessels.

Wade, 1724.

Cromwell's vessel was built in Inverness and transported overland, but Wade's was constructed on the banks of Loch Ness itself. The galley was about thirty tons and used principally to move men and equipment between Fort Augustus and Inverness.

Weth she made her first trip she was mightily adorned with colours, and fired her guns several times, which was a strange sight to the Highlanders, who had never seen the like before.

Cameron Lees, 1897, p128.

Wade's programme of inspection and his report are regarded as showing shrewd insights and analysis. He made thorough and close observations of the prevailing circumstances, he sifted reliable from biased opinions (including progressively distancing himself from Lord Lovat as he began to realise that Simon Fraser was not an honourable man) and he brought to bear his earlier military and geographical knowledge to demonstrate in his report that good communication is essential for successful stewardship.

Before I conclude this Report, I presume to observe to your Maty, the great Disadvantages Regular Troops are under when they engage with those who Inhabit Mountainous Situations. The Sevennes in France, and Catalans in Spain have in all times been instances of this truth.

Although it is unlikely that Wade saw a complex of military roads in the Highlands as early as the time of his December 1724 report, the beginnings of this idea must have been forming in his mind. His own roots had sent him from living in a rural environment into the military. His developed skills as a soldier and leader helped him to understand the motives and fears of those facing acute confrontation and the shame of submitting to blackmail in near 'no-go areas'. His first-hand experience of fighting in difficult terrain must have pressed home to him the advantages to be had for troops moving speedily across well laid routes and tracks. Taken together, these influences probably sparked the idea that a co-ordinated and effective transportation system was the foundation for fair and steadfast policing.

Whatever the exact pattern of influences, and whenever the full picture of a pattern of 'mountain roads' emerged in his thinking, his labour over the best part of the next decade was to secure a defined road network through some of the remotest parts of the Scottish Highlands.

Reports to roads

THE GOVERNMENT acted quickly on Wade's recommendations. On Christmas Eve 1724 he was appointed commander-in-chief, North Britain. Within the remit of this post he offered proposals in the spring of 1725. He estimated he would need six regiments of foot in Scotland; two of these to garrison the forts and barracks in the Highlands. His financial estimate was £10,000 a year for two years. This estimate included

4 From paper to pathway

money to build the *Highland Galley*, cash to construct the new forts at Killichuimen and Inverness, and finance for

> mending the Roads between the Garrisons and Barracks, for the better Communication of his Majesty's Troops.

> *Wade, 1725.*

The government gave its support to Wade's proposals. He received £5,000 on account for the current year and this money included that needed to

> defray charges... for repairing the roads between the garrisons and barracks.

> *Quoted in Salmond, 1934.*

In discharging his responsibilities as commander-in-chief, Wade's reliability and practical good sense came well to the fore. For example, his thorough preparations enabled a sizeable force to be in place quickly at Inverness, the consequence being that around fifty clan chieftains made their peace with the crown. He did not offend the pride of the lairds, accepting their arms direct to him without the presence of the established Highland companies. They 'thought it more consistent with their honour to resign their arms to Your Majesty's veteran troops; to which I readily consented'.

When the weather permitted purposeful work to be done, his road repair and road building programme proceeded efficiently. Progress was no doubt enhanced because the troops engaged in the work were generally treated well, and

> the Non-Commission Officers and Soldiers are allow'd double pay during the time they are employed in this Service.

> *Wade report to George II, 1728.*

In later years, well after the deaths of Wade and Caulfield, pay and conditions had declined significantly for the troops engaged in Highland road construction and repair. This we have on the witness of no less an observer than Dr Samuel Johnson. On his 1773 journey to the Western Isles he came upon a party of soldiers just beyond Fort Augustus. They were 'working on the road, under the superintendence of a serjeant'. Such was the poorness of their circumstances and the demands of their toil that he gave them some money. He stayed that night in Anoch and encountered the road-making party again at his inn.

> They had the true military impatience of coin in their pockets, and had marched at least six miles to find the first place where liquor could be bought... . All that we gave them was not much, but it detained them in the barn, either

merry or quarrelling the whole night, and in the morning they went back to their work with great indignation at the bad qualities of whisky.

Johnson, 1785, quoted in Allan, 1925.

Historical connection 3

Perhaps Dr Johnson overemphasises the 'true military impatience of coin in their pockets' and underplays the 'relief' such 'wealth' allowed from the rigours of working in Scotland's harsh physical terrain and climate. Others have made similar journeys at worse consequences to themselves; for example, the workers constructing the Blackwater dam high above Kinlochleven (1904–09). Several of these men traversed terrain as demanding as the 'Devil's Staircase', some at the cost of their lives, for the distinct relief that partaking of the local refreshment provided.

> There was a graveyard in the place, and a few went there... with the red muck on their trousers and their long unshaven beards still on their faces. Maybe they died on a journey, or under a fallen rock or a broken derrick jib. Once dead they were buried, and there was an end of them.
>
> *Macgill, 1985, pp214–15.*

Another example of Wade's pragmatism was his vigilance about Jacobitism. His intelligence service monitored Jacobite designs and a report by him in 1772 on possible activities in favour of the Pretender resulted in three speedy actions. First, some further strengthening of the garrisons at Edinburgh and Stirling Castles. Second, an increase in the size of the Highland companies. Third, more money for road works.

The revitalised concern about Jacobite intentions also allowed Wade a platform from which to draw the government's attention to the poor condition of the forts and castles used to house the troops. To make his point, Wade had four soldiers at Edinburgh take on full equipment and exit and enter the castle to test its defences. By this practical experiment he was able to report that

> they performed with such Dexterity; That from the Common Road, they mounted into the Castle in less than five minutes.

Wade's second report. Sent to George II in 1728.
From Historical Papers, *Spalding Club.*

By both his vigilance and his eye for clear demonstration, Wade earned from the crown £7,000 in each of the years 1727 and 1728 for repairing barracks and fortifications.

From the beginning, in order to sustain his claims for continuing income, Wade provides regular and graphic correspondence about the programme of road building. He is wise enough in these communications to play the now commonplace trusty cards of favourable public relations, prudent project management and compliance with the goals of central policy. He does this by outlining the local benefits arising from improved communication, by carefully listing all controlled expenditure and by highlighting the contribution the programme makes to the retention of the crown's supremacy. For example, in 1726, when writing about his recent decision to enlarge the new road between Killichuimen and Fort William, and to lay a good coach road between Fort William and Inverness, he says

> the work is carried on by the Military with less expense and difficulty than I first imagined it could be performed; and the Highlanders, from the ease and conveniency of transporting their merchandise, begin to approve and applaud what they had first repined and submitted to with reluctancy.

> *Wade's letter to Lord Townshend, dated 16th September 1726.*

In 1727 he indicates that a road

> 'may be continued to Perth at very moderate
> expense by the regiments quartered in these
> parts', and in a number of his correspondences
> he refers to the contribution the roads and
> barracks will play in 'preventing or suppressing
> insurrections'.

> *Wade's letter to Lord Townshend,*
> *written early in 1727.*

The Treasury did continue to advance money, so road making went on a pace in the years 1726 to 1738. George I died on 11th June 1727, but George II supported Wade's commission. It is likely that the regularity and clarity of Wade's reports and accounts did find favour with those advising the different occupants of the throne. This, despite the fact that Wade often reports

> 'amounts in the whole' to be 'more than the
> net produce' of the respective 'Majesty's
> warrant'.

> *Treasury papers numbers 24 and 31.*

Overall, though, the maintenance of the commission lies essentially in the continuing belief at that time that any roads through the barren mountainous terrain of the Highlands, which made wheel carriage 'easy and practicable', was the key to suppressing any tendencies in favour of the Jacobite cause.

It is also equally likely that those staff in the Treasury of the period had some idea that Wade was delivering value for money. This value is borne out by a summary of payments made to Wade between 1728 and 1737. These payments are listed in the respective *King's Warrant Book*. They total to £23,316 0s 6d, of which £16,000 is direct spending on 240 miles of road. This is about seventy pounds per mile. What the final sixpence in the grant actually provided is open to speculation. However, a close scrutiny of the accounts suggests that the pence arithmetic is not entirely accurate.

Wade called his soldier-toilers 'highwaymen'. That is, men performing 'their part on ye Highways'. They worked with simple tools, such as the '94 Shovells, 82 Pickaxes, forty two Spades and 3 Iron Crows' ordered by Wade from Edinburgh Castle in 1726, though dynamite was used to break up the largest boulders.

5 Highwaymen at their toil.

Other sizeable rocks were 'shifted' out of the way, sometimes with severe consequences for the mental well-being of the local folk.

> The first design of removing a vast fallen piece of rock was entertained by the country people with great derision, of which I saw one instance myself. A very old wrinkled Highland woman upon such an occasion, standing over against me when the soldiers were fixing their engines, seemed to sneer at it, and said something to an officer of the Highland companies. I imagined she was making a jest of the undertaking, and asked the officer what she had said. 'I will tell you her words,' said he. 'What are the fools doing? That stone will lie there for ever, for all of them;' but when she saw that vast bulk begin to rise, though by slow degrees, she set up a hideous Irish yell, took to her heels, ran up the side of the hill just like a young girl, and never looked behind her while she was in our sight. I make no doubt she thought it was magic and the workmen warlocks.
>
> *Cameron Lees, p131.*

The early roads went the Roman way – built when possible in a straight line – and tending therefore to go over rather than around high ground. Zigzags underpinned by bulwarks of stone and mortar traversed steepness. The roads were generally of good width (about sixteen feet) and like the fell footpaths of today they had piles of marker stones to help with direction in poor visibility and to help the traveller during harsh winters. Edmund Burt in his *Letters* paints a picture of the roads that shows how difficult the navigation would be in less than perfect conditions:

> The standard breadth of these roads, as laid down at the first projection, is sixteen feet; but in some parts, where there were no very expensive difficulties, they are wider.

> In those places… they are carried on in straight lines till some great necessity has turned them out of the way; the rest, which run along in declivities of hills… have their circuits, risings, and descents accordingly.

> To stop and take a general view of the hills before you from an eminence, in some part where the eye penetrates far within the void spaces, the roads would appear to you in a kind of whimsical disorder; and as those parts of them that appear to you are of a very different colour from the heath that chiefly clothes the country, they may, by that contrast, be traced out to a considerable distance.

Now, let us suppose that where you are, the road is visible to you for a short space, and is then broken off to the right by a hollow or winding among the hills; beyond that interruption, the eye catches a small part on the side of another hill, and some again on the ridge of it; in another place, further off, the road appears to run zigzag, in angles, up a steep declivity; in one place, a short horizontal line shows itself below, in another, the marks of the road seem to be almost even with the clouds, etc.

Burt's letter XXVI in Simmons (ed), 1998, p281.

Historical connection 4

The military roads did not always proceed by innovatory routes. They often followed some line or rough track that had been in place for centuries. Even the road over the Corrieyairack pass, though commonly referred to as 'Wade's Military Road', was probably a former cattle drive or drove road and it had certainly seen earlier military use than the 1745 Jacobite advance. For example,

in February 1645, during the Covenanting wars, Montrose trapped

---

between a force of 5000 men at Inverness and 3000 Campbells at Inveraray, took his 1500 men from Fort Augustus over the Corrieyairack in deep snow before doubling back along Glen Roy and down to Inverlochy, where the unprepared Campbells were comprehensively slaughtered.

Dunn, 1986, p216.

Overall, however, Wade's roads

followed routes not extensively used by cattle which, in any event, did not keep to a narrow track.

Haldane, 1997.

When the roads were first constructed, no bridges were built. Suitable places were selected for fording rivers and burns. All loose stones were cleared away, and in some places a causeway was made. Of course, this meant continual labour, as each new spate brought fresh stones into the ford. Wooden bridges were constructed as soon as circumstances permitted, and in time stone arches replaced these. The well known Tay Bridge at Aberfeldy was not completed until 1735, well into the second part of Wade's road and bridge building schedule.

6 *Some original bridges remain on the military roads.*

Being constructed in an age before asphalt and tar, the roads were made from raw materials gathered from the local surroundings. The design of the road was, by modern standards, decidedly simple. Trench-style foundations were dug and filled with big stones. Much sledge-hammering made smaller stones and these formed the next layer. The small stones were covered with gravel up to a thickness of about two feet, and the surface was then beaten with shovels and stamped on with feet. Heavily laden carts (usually those bringing gravel from nearby hillsides) provided a 'steam-roller' effect for final levelling. Open-paved drains went across the surface at various points, to carry away descending water, and if the ground was especially soft or marshy,

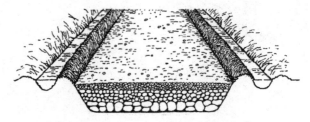

8 A transection of a 'typical' Wade road.

the roads were constructed on a foundation of brushwood and roughly hewn timber.

Like their modern counterparts, Wade's roads suffered from natural and human erosion. Replacement of top gravel, easily washed away by surface or loch water, was a frequent necessity, and shortly after construction of one of the roads, Perthshire had to publish an order instructing that they 'were made for wheel carriages and

1 Caulfield's 'White Bridge' near Tyndrum.

2 Protection at last for these
famous roads
3 The protection notice
4 A Wade road starts at Fort
Augustus (top right)
5 Black Watch Memorial at
Aberfeldy (bottom right)

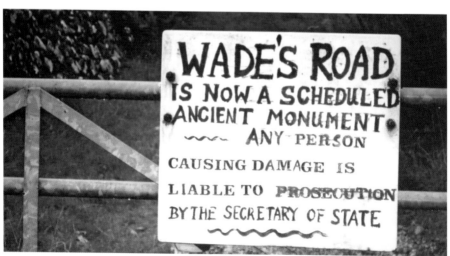

6 *Winding down from Lagan to Fort Augustus.*

7 *Bonnie Prince Charlie reflects at Derby.*

were greatly deteriorated by other practices' (such as local folk dragging trees along them).

> These roads... tho' ever so well made, will be very soon destroyed if some method is not found or somehow made to prevent the trailing of deal boards and fir timbers along them. The country people trail these deals and timbers in very great quantity... to their markets and villages... tearing away all the gravel and making channels for the rain water, which thus gathers into currents and destroys all before them, especially on the descents and sides of the hills.
>
> *Source unknown, but quoted in*
> *Bullock, 1931, p5.*

Although Wade fathered the idea of a network of military roads in the Highlands, he returned south on a number of occasions for parliamentary and other business. His southern excursions increased in the 1730s, and it is likely that he was not in Scotland at any time in the year 1739. The following year (1740) he left the Highlands to take up other duties. Fortunately for the development of the road project, he had appointed in 1732 William Caulfield to be his inspector of roads. Caulfield outlived Wade and stayed with military road building until his death in 1767.

There is still some controversy about which man was

responsible for which parts of the early sections, but it is generally accepted that William built many more miles of road than George. Wade is estimated to have overseen the construction of about 258 miles, Caulfield over three times that length – circa 800-plus miles (the exact mileage is not known). In truth, the matter is perhaps best left as one for academic speculation only. Each man respected the other. Wade found Caulfield to be a reliable inspector and surveyor. Caulfield named his eldest son Wade Toby and there is some belief that William himself was the author of the oft-quoted verse:

> If you had seen these roads before they were
> made
> You would hold up your hands and bless
> General Wade.

It is known that both men enjoyed 'bumpers', though Wade's reputation as a soldier who was well able to manage his deportment when it came to drink, suggests it is unlikely he would have needed to use Caulfield's 'cradle'. The 'cradle' was installed in Caulfield's house – Cradlehall at Inverness – and was a crude form of lift by which inebriated guests were hoisted by block and tackle from the hall to an upper floor – and so to bed!

By 1757 Caulfield had spent £130,000 on his roads. Lieutenant Colonel Skene succeeded him in the position of inspector. Skene took over 858 miles of military highway, with another 140 miles under construction. By

1784, the commander of the forces in Scotland, Lieutenant-General Mackay, reported to the Treasury that the military roads in the Highlands amounted to about 1,100 miles. He goes on in his report to inform that many are in a state of bad repair. He proposes to cease further maintenance of some from the public purse, and to put out to 'contract hire' the horses and carts used for conveyancing. He accuses the by now 'contract workmen' of having acted 'improperly' and he asks for an overseer to work under the inspector. By 1799 only 599 miles of the network was being kept in repair. By 1812, only those as 'might be useful to the public' were maintained in any sort of reasonable order. The future had caught up with the military roads. The increasing volume of civilian traffic, now travelling by stagecoach and more comfortable wheeled carts, found the military roads too difficult.

> Lady Seaforth once endeavoured to take her carriage over it [the military road from Inverness to Ruthven], but the whole equipage broke down.

Sir Kenneth Mackenzie in Bullock (op cit), p20.

In time then, the military roads lost out as the chief routes of communication – first, as the military presence in the Highlands was scaled down; second, as those engineers with better road building techniques (for example, Thomas Telford) sought routes that did not go over steep fells, and did not pose the challenge of 'major realignment' in order to straighten a difficult bend.

Historical connection 5

The difficulties faced by the soldier road-builders and the rapid deterioration of their finished product is evidenced in the travels of John Stanhope and Archibald Macdonald.

In 1806, after spending a night at a former house built by Wade and in use by 1806 as the Dalwhinnie Inn, they set off to cross the Corrieyairack Mountain by using Wade's road to Fort Augustus. Stanhope has left in his diary this vivid impression of what they experienced:

> The road was execrable and we picked our way with difficulty. In a short time we found ourselves at the foot of the long-dreaded Corryarrick. It was six miles to the top of it and three down the other side. With all the spirit that our wet and frozen limbs permitted we began to ascend. The road was a zigzag, the surface covered with large, loose stones and every now and then it degenerated into steps cut through a rock. Thus we staggered on, in the middle of a dreadful rain, abetted by a

---

most violent wind, so that we were wet
to the skin and frozen in numbness by
the sharpness of the gale.

They found the challenges beyond Fort Augustus
even more daunting:

There had once, I believe been a road...
made by General Wade. It was composed
of rocks and loose stones, and variegated
with rivers and bogs which the great
quantity of rain that had fallen rendered
very deep and dangerous.

Cooper and Godwin, p27.

Regiments. and rebellions

THROUGHOUT THE period of his commission in Scotland, Wade remained alert to the possibility of another Jacobite rising. His preventative strategy was twofold. First, he continued to strengthen the Highland companies and their fortresses. In doing so he tried to purge these companies of any men thought to be of Jacobite susceptibility, and he used the loyal companies from time to time to search for caches of weapons. Second, he tried to stay on good terms with clan chiefs, principally by adopting a paternalist approach to their interests and possible Jacobite leanings.

The available evidence leads to uncertainty on the success of these strategies. Following a rumour of emissaries sent to encourage support for a Spanish landing in favour of the Stuart cause, Wade ordered a weapons search, but it was unsuccessful. He reports that none were discovered except about twenty muskets that had been hid in a cave ever since the Highlands were disarmed in 1725, and these had grown so rusty that they were entirely unfit for service.

Wade's report to George II, 1728.

He made some arrests but those thought to be principally behind the support for the Spanish intention escaped. His talks with some of the chiefs led him to conclude

they had suffered sufficiently for their past folly, but were now determined to live peacefully and quietly, and hoped by their future good behaviour to deserve Your Majesty's Favour and Protection.

Wade report to George II.

From such evidence one could incline to a view that Wade misjudged the continuing undercurrent of Jacobite plotting and had misplaced faith in the results of the disarmament strategy. Or, it is equally plausible to view the evidence as indicating a significant lull in Jacobitism, possibly begun and sustained by Wade's presence in the Highlands, thereby keeping plots and would-be rebels in a fairly dormant state until the 1738 English Jacobite Council and the resurgence behind Charles Edward Stuart in 1744. The clear fact is that Wade did not renege on his responsibilities. He obeyed distasteful and repressive instructions, but in general the disarming proceeded so slowly and so judiciously, that his obedience to these orders did not make him unpopular.

Wade tapped those clans known to be loyal to the government for military recruitment. He supported the idea of arming these loyal groups and this led to men from the Campbell, Grant, Fraser, and Munro clans becoming the backbone of the first regiment of 'Black Watch'. The name derives from the dark tartan they wore to distinguish them from the 'Red' Guards Company, and because they had a special responsibility to keep a 'watch' on the Highlands. To enable them to carry out this responsibility to good effect, they were posted throughout the Highlands, excepting only those areas regarded by the crown as decidedly peaceful.

Historical connection 6

By 1739 the Black Watch were formed into a regular regiment, the 43rd, and had an establishment of 815 men. Historical folklore holds that the plaid of a sergeant from the 43rd serving with Fraser's Highlanders at Quebec was used to carry the mortally wounded General Wolfe to the rear of the battlefield and this same sergeant, one Donald Macleod, was in the guard that escorted Wolfe's body on its voyage to England. Macleod it is said served for seventy-one years in the army and fought in at least six great battles. He was badly wounded at least five times and shipwrecked once. Despite these adversities he did not retire from the army until 88 years of age and lived on to reach 103. This considerable record of service has some historical credence (Barnes, undated publication.)

When absorbed in the regular army, the Black Watch troops were allowed to retain their traditional name and dress. They became the 42nd or Highland Regiment in 1749 and the Royal Highland Regiment in 1758. A memorial acknowledging the foundation of this now famous regiment stands near to Wade's most notable achievement, the Tay Bridge at Aberfeldy.

In June 1727, three regiments of dragoons increased the military presence in Scotland. Wade, who had been promoted to lieutenant general in March of that year, received the colonelcy of one of these three regiments. By 1733, he had become governor of the three new forts – Augustus, George and William. Records of his annual military reviews show a continuance in military strength throughout the 1730s, so that by 1738 the presence was at least 3,000 foot and some 600 horses.

8 Aberfeldy Bridge.

The year 1739 also saw Wade's promotion to general. In 1740 he relinquished the command in Scotland, later becoming commander-in-chief of British forces in Flanders (in 1743). His fate in the subsequent Austrian, Dutch and British conflagration with the French is well recorded.

When the campaign opened in 1744, Wade was seventy years of age, in failing health, and he had never commanded a full army in the field. His plans were opposed by the Austrian and Dutch commanders, no definite plan of action for the campaign emerged, and despite expected superiority in the allied numbers and formation, the French made significant gains in the first six weeks.

An officer serving with the allies notes the lack of campaign strategy. He wrote home:

> the ability of M. de Saxe [Maurice of Saxe, French commander] is such that he manoeuvres our army as well as his own.
>
> Gent Mag, *1744.*

The extent of the French success led to Lord Carteret informing Wade that:

> it was his majesty's pleasure the army should march upon the enemy and attack him with a spirit suitable to the glory of the British Nation.
>
> *Carteret mss.*

To confound Wade's chances of meeting this request, he was now required to follow a plan of campaign prepared in England by the earl of Stair. Stair knew little or nothing about the situation in the field, and disorganisation continued. A reduced French army positioned behind the Lys saw to it that the allies again achieved no headway.

By this time, Wade was the butt of French cartoons and dramatic sketches, and early in October his health broke down. His request for leave to return to England was granted and in 1745 he resigned his command. The letter accepting his resignation lays no blame at his door for the Flanders fiasco. It includes a statement that:

> his Majesty was pleased to express ye most perfect Satisfaction in your past Services
>
> *Mahon.*

and the king later declared faith in Wade by making him commander-in-chief in England, albeit Wade held this status for only a very short period of time.

The 'forty-five rising' brought Wade back to the battlefield.

9 Redcoats and Highlanders in conflict again.

He took to the offensive with the forces he could collect (a mixture of troops recalled from Flanders and a sizeable number of Dutch troops).

Historical connection 7

One of the officers who served with Wade in Flanders and in pursuit of the Jacobites was James Wolfe, later General Wolfe of Quebec fame. He was a newly appointed adjutant when he went into winter quarters with Wade at Ostend in 1743. After Wade had been recalled in October 1744, Wolfe served with Sir John Ligonier until the duke of Cumberland took over in Flanders in February 1745. By 12th June 1745, Cumberland was signing Wolfe's commission as brigade major.

With the early Jacobite advances from July 1745, the government set about recalling regiments from Flanders. Orders were sent to Cumberland in September

> requiring him to send ten battalions home immediately
>
> *Reid, 2000, p63.*

The exact date James Wolfe came is uncertain, but Wade signed for

---

> Major Wolfe to be paid £930 for... 93 baggage horses to the seven battalions lately come from Flanders.
>
> *Reid, op cit, p64.*
>
> Wolfe later served with Lieutenant General Henry Hawley against the Jacobites at Falkirk Moor, and finally at Culloden. As the hero of Quebec, he died on the Plains of Abraham on 13th September 1759.

By September 1745, Wade had concentrated his army at Newcastle. Prince Charlie's force, in the throes of their victory at Prestopans, made false trails to meet Wade, but then turned suddenly westward, marched into Cumberland and captured Carlisle.

Once acquainted with the outmanoeuvre, Wade attempted to meet with the Jacobite forces, but because of snowstorms – and, ironically, bad roads – he only reached Hexham. The roads became impassable, stopping any further march westward by him. He returned to Newcastle as Charles Edward continued his victorious journey, now south to Derby. The duke of Cumberland with a fresh army of 8,000 men set out to meet the rebels. For Wade the jibes of Flanders returned.

And pray, who is so fit to lead forth this parade,
As the babe of Tangier, My old grandmother Wade?
Whose cunning so quick, but whose motion
    so slow,
That the rebels march'd on, while he stuck in snow.

Wade papers, held originally by the Junior United
Services Club, but now probably lost.

Historical connection 8

Derby's link with Bonnie Prince Charlie's army began at about 11 a.m. on 4th December 1745. Two officers arrived demanding billets for the men. The rest of the army arrived through Sadler Gate and gathered in the market place.

They were

> a mixture of every rank, from childhood
> to old age, from the dwarf to the giant,
> chiefly in deranged dresses, marked by
> dirt and fatigue.... They were ushered
> in by the bagpipes.
>
> *Childs, 1986, p39.*

Prince Charles Edward chose the Tory marquess of Exeter's enormous house for his headquarters. The house has not survived, but the original oak panelling from it now forms a backcloth for the 'The Bonnie Prince Charlie Room' at Derby Museum.

The Pretender's commanders and his court were billeted in nearby alderman's residences or town houses. The army made do as best they could.

Although the exact size of the army is not known, it was near equal to, or in excess of, the total population of Derby at the time. (Population of Derby in 1745 was at about 6,000; Highlander army said to be between 5,000 and 9,000 men in strength.) The impact then on the city of this sizeable force of men, with their different language and costume, must have been significant and for a brief time an anxious threat to the locality.

It was however a brief affair. The prince's war council met in the panelled drawing room at Exeter House on 5th December. They would not support going further south. Lord George Murray, son of the first duke of Atholl, pointed to three great obstacles. The estimated strength and location of the opposing forces, the unlikelihood of an English rising, and the improbability of further reinforcements from Scotland. He and others pressed the case for a new offensive in the spring. The disillusioned Jacobite army thus reluctantly decided on 6th December to turn around for the border.

The prince's highlander army now faced the troops of both Wade and Cumberland, but they got safely between these two armies and back through the county of Cumberland (now Cumbria) into Scotland. Their final fate at the battle of Culloden is well known.

Cumberland took over as commander-in-chief of the whole British army and Wade retired to civilian life. Now seventy-three years old, he made his last significant public appearance as the president of the board of general officers who investigated the conduct of Sir John Cope.

Cope had the opportunity in August 1745 to engage the Jacobite army at the Corrieyairack Pass. He halted at Dalwhinnie on receipt of information that he was outnumbered by the rebels who were 'entrenched to their teeth' (Kemp, 1975, p7) along the adjacent summits. Cope's council of war decided to turn aside to Inverness, there to gather reinforcements. Although this was a forward movement, Edinburgh and the Lowlands now lay open to the Jacobites. They did not pursue Cope north, but availed themselves of the opportunity to take Edinburgh.

Cope sailed his troops from Aberdeen to Dunbar and sought to relieve the city. The ensuing battle (named Prestopans, after a village to the rear of Cope's position, but called Gladsmuir by the Jacobites) left Cope retreating to Berwick with fewer than 450 men. Lord Mark Ler received him with the words

He believed he was the first general in Europe who had brought the first tidings of his own defeat.

Fairweather, p29.

10 Corrieyairack and Prestopans.

The subsequent 'enquiry' (it was not a court martial) must have reminded Wade of his time on the 'Corrieyairack' and the advantages secured into high ground by his road – albeit that in this case the enemy got to it more speedily than his majesty's colours.

Wade presided over exoneration. The trial concluded:

> That his (Cope's) attacking the rebels on the Corriarrick with any prospect of success, was impracticable... that his march to Inverness was justified by the unanimous opinion of the Council of War... and by assurances of being joined on the march by clans reputed to be well affected to your Majesty... that his going by sea to Dunbar was the only proper measure... left to take... that the Disposition of his Body of Troops was judicious and the Ground... well chosen... that he did his duty as an officer both before, at, and after the Action... and Misfortune of the Day was owing to the Shameful Behaviour of the Private Men... Cope's behaviour has been blameless.
>
> *(GCT (1749) 'Report of the Examination into the conduct of General Sir John Cope, Colonel P. Lascelles and General T. Fowke in the rebellion in North Britain in 1745.'*

The report is covered extensively in Cadell (1898).

Military historians are still engaged in debate about the fairness of this judgement, but poor 'Johnny Cope' has long since passed into a figure of fun in some folk songs. In general, however, there is much evidence that points to the board having made a fair decision.

First, Cope had only a small force of mercenaries and relatively inexperienced soldiers, as the flower of the British army was still on the continent. Second, the Jacobite army did possess very high ground overlooking a near impregnable pass. Third, Charles Edward held twenty small canons brought from the *Doutelle* (sometimes also written as *Du Teillay*), the vessel he had sailed in from France, while Cope had only light guns and no artillerymen. Fourth, the government had ignored Cope's earlier requests for reinforcements in the Highlands, and finally, there was too much optimism that clans loyal to the crown would quickly join Cope's army.

George Wade did not return to any features of military life. He died in Bath on 14th March 1748 at the age of seventy-five. He never married but he did father children. He left most of his considerable fortune (about £100,000) to his two sons William and John (both captains in the army) and to a daughter, Jane Erle. He provided generously for the widow and children of his brother William (formerly canon of Windsor).

In his will, dated 1st June 1747, Wade left £500 for the crafting and erection of a monument to himself. This was to be placed either in Bath Abbey or Westminster

Abbey. The sculptor Roubiliac completed the work at Westminster in 1750. He regarded it as his 'best work' and it is said that he used to come and stand before it and weep because he thought it placed too high for good appreciation.

Roubiliac's reputation was established with the completion of a marble statue of the composer George Friedrich Handel. The new proprietor of Vauxhall Gardens, Jonathan Tyers, for whom Roubiliac also completed a work of John Milton, commissioned this work. The statue of Handel was erected in April 1738 and shows the great composer in informal pose. He is leaning on copies of his recent works and holding a lyre.

In the 1750s Roubiliac received many commissions, including one from the actor David Garrick for a marble statue of William Shakespeare.

His reputation grew both through his work on monuments for Westminster Abbey and by the bestowal of favourable comments from established dignitaries. For example, in 1771, John Wesley praised his monument in Westminster Abbey to Joseph and Elizabeth Nightingale.

Although Roubiliac himself thought that his monument to Marshal George Wade was among his very best work, others have been less generous. Dean Stanley stated in 1868 that visitors to Westminster Abbey would

> pass with scorn the enormous structures which Roubiliac raised in the Nave to General Wade and General Hargrave
>
> *Macmillan, 1996, p244.*

 *Reflections*

SO WHAT personal qualities of George Wade can we deduce from his life? What were his main talents and achievements?

His contribution to improving communication in the Highlands is now well respected. He had no blueprint and little preceding experience to guide him. Essentially, he devised his own approach and knew that it had to be one that operated principally not through the deployment of skilled craftsmen, but through the labours of serving soldiers. Later, some stonemasons were employed on bridge building, but initially, the cartography, forward planning, traverses and basic engineering came from Wade's own belief that a system of roads could be placed in the remoter Highland areas.

He served conscientiously as an MP for two English constituencies: Hindon in Wiltshire, but more significantly in the city of Bath. In general he was straightforward and honest, and when he was faced with

a job he got it done. He headed many charities in the
Bath area and contributed money to local church
building and local slum clearance.

12 Wade's house at Bath.

Historical connection 10

The National Trust in Bath now occupies Wade's Georgian House. The exterior remains impressive but little of the interior is available to visitors.

Wade also owned other houses and one of these has passed into historical folklore. He succumbed like many in his time to the presence of the 'amateur architect'. One of the leading Palladian architects was Lord Burlington who designed a London house for him.

Wade found it irritating and not comfortable. On proclaiming this he was advised by Lord Chesterfield to

> take a house on the opposite side of the road and look at his own.
>
> *Quennell and Quennell, 1950.*

As a soldier Wade has been described as more solid than brilliant, and some have suggested he was not fit for successful command. He certainly had grave misfortunes in the closing stages of his military career, but he was encumbered in both Flanders and during the 1745

Jacobite action, with political and military confusion, advancing age, ill health and other extenuating circumstances. In particular, the overall command in Flanders, though collaborative, was indecisive and ineffective, and the perplexing and contradictory reports about a Jacobite army that was reforming and expanding as it marched, teased the best military intelligence of the day.

In contrast to this late period of his service, his early military career shows a decisive leader with courage and initiative. As commander-in-chief, North Britain, he lacked neither ideas nor respect. He may have been kindly disposed to his men and the consequences for them of harsh physical conditions and military conflagration, and in demonstrating this quality he contrasts sharply with the other chief commander of the day, the infamous duke of Cumberland.

The more general evidence about Wade from correspondence and press extracts presents him as a compassionate man. A letter to him from Catherine Allardice pleading for his support for the reprieve of Captain Porteous acknowledges qualities in him of generosity and goodwill to his fellows. These seem to be genuine recognition of his attributes and not just a form of flattery from someone wishing to secure his influence.

Historical connection 11

Captain Jack Porteous, also known as Black Jock Porteous, was captain of the Edinburgh city guard on 14th April 1736 when a smuggler, one Andrew Wilson, was executed. Wilson and a colleague named Robertson were arrested for robbing a collector of customs,

> an official as much detested as his assailants' occupation was admired throughout Scotland.
>
> *Stuart, 1960, p278.*

Before, during and after the execution, the crowd became very agitated and turned their wrath on the city guard. Porteous is said to have fired a musket shot into the crowd, though he himself denied this. It seems clear, however, that either by order or default, about fourteen members of the guard did fire on the people. Although estimates of casualties vary, the most reliable sources point to six onlookers killed and eleven wounded.

Porteous was arrested for murder, tried and sentenced for execution on 8th September. Queen Caroline, who was at the time guardian of the realm, took in to account Wade's request for clemency and respited Porteous for six weeks.

The people of Edinburgh hotly resented the granting of the respite and on the eve prior to the day originally set for Porteous's execution, an armed body of men in disguise broke into the prison, seized Porteous and hanged him on a signpost in the street. It was intimated that persons of high status were involved in the crime.

Such an outrage by the public could not be ignored. An official enquiry was established, but the body achieved little in the face of a conspiracy of silence. Although three acts of retribution were passed – first, that all ministers should publicly invite their congregations to 'discover' Porteous's murderers; second, that Edinburgh be fined £2,000 in recompense; and third that the lord provost be removed from holding office – only the last two reached fruition. The £2,000 was assigned to Porteous's widow and another man called Wilson was removed (albeit this was Lord Provost Wilson and only from his office).

The murder of the unfortunate Captain Porteous provides the historical starting point for Sir Walter Scott's story, *The Heart of Midlothian*. The incident provides an initial backcloth for the very heart of the novel, an examination of the nature of justice itself.

Wade's compassion also came through in other ways. He twice secured a pardon for one John Smith, a sentinel sentenced to death for desertion. Unfortunately, poor Smith was not capable of returning the faith. He went 'one retreat too far' as shown in an Edinburgh newsprint dated 27th March 1730. This reads:

> On Thursday, John Smith, Centinel in Montague's Regiment was shot for Desertion. In his last words he acknowledged his having been twice pardoned by General Wade for the Like offence.

A compassionate nature is also attributed to Wade through an anecdote provided by Sir Horace Walpole. In a letter to Sir Horace Mann he writes:

> General Wade was at a low gaming-house, and had a very fine snuff-box, which on a sudden he missed. Everybody denied having taken it... he insisted on searching the company... he did until there remained only one man, who stood behind him, but refused to be searched, unless the General would go into another room alone with him... there the man told him, that he was born a gentleman, was reduced, and lived by what little bets he could pick up there, and

by the fragments which the waiters sometimes gave him.

'At this moment I have a half a fowl in my pocket; I was afraid of being exposed... here it is. Now Sir, you may search me.'

Wade was so struck that he gave the man a hundred pounds... and immediately the genius of the generosity, whose province is almost a sinecure, was very glad of the opportunity of making him find his own snuff box, or another very like it, in his own pocket again.

Salmond, op cit, p196.

Overwhelmingly, however, the evidence of Wade's compassion and care can be deduced from his treatment of 'his highwaymen'. He presents as a sensitive and caring leader of these soldiers. He had good rapport with them, he secured for these troops conditions and equipment well beyond the typical allocations of the day, and he ensured they celebrated completing sections of the roads with 'bonfire, roasts and good beverage'.

That Wade took on a difficult task in Scotland is beyond dispute. He made considerable progress in meeting the expectations of his commission without incurring extensive ill will. His skills and temperament appear to have been admired by friend and foe alike.

Much admiration of his work is expressed in verse.

When therefore, he is dead and gone,
Let this be writ upon his stone.
He never liked the narrow road,
But ran the king's high way to God.

From a poem dedicated to General Wade, circa 1737.

Still shall his living greatness guard his name
And his works lift him to immortal fame
Then shall astonished armies marching high
Over causewayed mountains that invade the sky
Climb the raised arch, that sweeps its distant
  throw
Cross tumbling floods, which roar ahead below
Gaze from the cliff's cut edge, through midway
  air,
And trembling, wonder on their safety there.

From a poem by Aaron Hill (1681–1750).

That Wade was skilful, and Wade was bold.
Thus shall his Fame, with George's glory rise,
Till Sun and Moon shall Tumble from the Skies.

Struan Robertson, Romantic Jacobite Laird, to
Edinburgh Gazette, *December 1735.*

Wade himself, though his payments for self-portraits and personal monuments suggest a degree of self-aggrandisement, speaks of his roads in more self-effacing terms. In one of his letters that has survived, he writes:

> If the goodness of the Highlands Roads and the convenience of the bridges has contributed to make your journey easy and pleasant, my ten years labour has not been in vain.

> *Wade letter to Lieutenant-General Clayton.*

To those who would say his roads breached the Highlands and took away the local autonomy, there is much evidence from the time to indicate that for many of the ordinary folk the parochial circumstances were those of serfdom and harsh treatment, under the rule of despotic lairds or the brutality of robber gangs. Those chiefs of the day, who regarded the road making as an irritant and a threat, tend to show motives primarily of self-interest and a desire to sustain the status quo.

> Those chiefs and other gentleman complain that thereby an easy passage is opened into the country for strangers, who in time, by their suggestions of liberty, will destroy or weaken the attachment of their vassals which it is so necessary for them to support and preserve.... . The lowest class, who many of them at some times cannot compass a pair of shoes for

themselves, allege that the gravel is intolerable for their naked feet; and the complaint has extended to their thin brogues. It is true they do sometimes for these reasons go without the road, and ride or walk in very commodious ways.

Cameron Lees, p132.

Inevitably such a despotic system could not last, and in opening up the Highlands, Wade only speeded up its demise.

If Wade's roads destroyed the power of the chiefs, it was a power that had to be destroyed sooner or later. Wade's attitude of mind towards the Highlands of Scotland was not that it was an area that should be subdued for the benefit of England, but a place that should be policed by its own people for its own good.

Salmond, 1934, p17.

So now Wade's and Caulfield's 'new roads' are but the 'old roads' on the map. They offer reflection and romance more than a route march, but they still pose challenging horizons and they still tire the feet. Armies continue to step out on them in varying weather and varying spirits, ironically mostly now to escape the 'civilisation' the roads once threatened to bring.

13 'I need these hills of freedom.'

The people love them and they use them for excursions into the remoter Scottish wilderness through which they renew their belief in themselves, their friendship with others, and their general health and happiness. Perhaps this use of the roads was always meant to be. It is nice to think that maybe Wade, Caulfield and the 'highwaymen' still watch over them, content in the knowledge that:

> In high, stony, and solitary places
> there is a strange market
> where you may barter the vortex of life
> for tranquillity of mind.
>
> *Milarepa.*

The principal events in George Wade's life

1673 Born third son of Jerome Wade of Killavalley, West Meath.

1690 Enters army. Ensign to Captain Richard Tevanian's company in the earl of Bath's regiment (10th Foot).

1691 Serves with his regiment at Steinkirk.

1692 Promoted to rank of lieutenant.

1702 Serves at the siege of Liege. His grenadiers greatly distinguish themselves in storming and carrying the citadel, one of the strongest fortifications in Flanders.

1703 Promoted major. Serves at the siege and capture of Huy.

1704 Brevet rank of colonel.

1706 Wounded at the siege of Alcantara but continues
to serve.

1707 Raised to the rank of major-general.

1715 Elected MP for Hindon, Wiltshire.

1722 MP for Bath (until 1748).

1725 Sent to pacify the Highlands in pursuance of the
'Act for Disarming the Highlands'.

1726 Most prolific period of his contribution
−34   to road building in Scotland.

1732 Governor of Berwick and Holy Island.

1733 Governor of Fort William, Fort Augusta and Fort
George (these retained until his death).

1739 Made a full general.

1740 Relieved of his command in Scotland.
(Succeeded by General Clayton.)

1742 Appointed lieutenant-general of the ordnance.

1743   Made field marshal.

1744   Commanded the British forces in Flanders.

1744   On outbreak of Jacobite rebellion set out to
       oppose the Pretender's forces. Pursued the rebels
       through Yorkshire, but considered to be too
       inactive and in consequence superseded in
       command by General Harley.

1748   Died 14th March. Buried in Westminster Abbey.

Bibliography

Allan, P (ed) *A Journey to the Western Isles of Scotland: Johnson's Journey to the Hebrides*, P Allan and Co, 1925.

Barnes, Major R Money, *The Uniforms and History of The Scottish Regiments: 1625 forward*, Seeley Service Ltd, London.

Brander, M, *The Making of the Highlands*, Guild Publishing, 1980.

Bullock, J M, *Old Highland Highways*, Inverness Publications, 1931.

Burt, E, *Letters from a Gentleman in the North of Scotland to His Friend in London* (fifth edition), William Paterson, Edinburgh, 1876.

Cadell, R, *Sir John Cope and the Rebellion of 1745*, Edinburgh and London, 1898.

Cameron Lees, J, *A History of the County of Inverness*, Blackwood and Sons, 1897.

Childs, J, *Stuart Derbyshire*, The Derbyshire Heritage Series, J H Hall and Sons, Derby, 1986.

Cooper, D and Godwin, F, *The Whisky Roads of Scotland*, Jill Norman and Hobhouse Ltd, 1982.

Dunn, M, *Walking Ancient Trackways*, David and Charles, London, 1986.

Fairweather, B, *The '45 Jacobite Rising*, The Glencoe and North Lorn Folk Museum.

Haldane, A R B, *The Drove Roads of Scotland*, Birlinn, 1997.

Johnson, S, *Journey to the Western Isles of Scotland*, 1785.

Kemp, H, *The Jacobite Rebellion*, Almark Publishing Co Ltd, 1975.

Macgill, P, *Children Of The Dead End*, Caliban Books, 1985.

Macmillan Publishers Ltd, *The Dictionary of Art*, vol 27, 1996.

Lord Mahon, *History of England 1713–1783* , Leipzig, Bernard Tauchnik.

Quennell, M and Quennell, C H B, *A History of Everyday Things in England (1500–1799)*, London, Batsford, 1950.

Randall, G, *Church Furnishing and Decoration in England and Wales*, London, Batsford, 1980.

Reid, S, *The Career of General James Wolfe from Culloden to Quebec*, Spellmount Ltd, 2000.

Salmond, J, *Wade in Scotland*, The Moray Press, 1934.

Simmons, A (ed), *Burt's Letters from the North of Scotland*, Birlinn Ltd, Edinburgh, 1998.

Stanhope, Earl, *History of England*.

Stuart, C H, *The Whig Supremacy (1714–1736)*, Oxford University Press, 1960.

Taylor, W, *The Military Roads in Scotland*, David and
Charles, 1976.

Wade, G, *General Wade's Report to King George 1 – 10
December 1724*. Printed as an appendix to the fifth
edition of Burt's *Letters*.

Wade, G, 'A "scheme" for disarming the highlands',
communication to King George I, April 1725.

Youngson, A, *The Highlands in the Eighteenth Century*,
Collins, 1974.